Raffi.

Shake my sillies
out.

$14.30

Preschool
04-1019

DATE			

Raffi Songs to Read®

SHAKE MY SILLIES OUT

Illustrated by David Allender

You Are Entering

MARIPOSA FOREST

BEWARE of SILLY ANIMALS

Crown Publishers, Inc., New York

For Justin and Joel

Published by Crown Publishers, Inc., a Random House company, 201 East 50th Street,
New York, New York 10022
CROWN is a trademark of Crown Publishers, Inc.
RAFFI SONGS TO READ and SONGS TO READ are registered trademarks of
Troubadour Learning, a division of Troubadour Records Ltd.
Manufactured in the United States of America

Library of Congress Cataloging-in-Publication Data
Raffi. Shake my sillies out. Summary: A trio of animals who can't get to sleep roam
the forest and eventually encounter a group of campers who join them in shaking
their sillies out, clapping their crazies out, and yawning their sleepies out.
1. Children's songs. [1. Songs] I. Simpson, Bert. II. Simpson, Bonnie, III. Title.
M1998.R   87-750478
ISBN 0-517-56646-X (trade)
       0-517-56647-8 (pbk.)   19 20

Originally published in hardcover in 1987
First paperback edition February 1990

Front photo copyright © 1987 David Street
Back photo copyright © 1987 Patrick Harbron

 This book is printed on chlorine-free paper

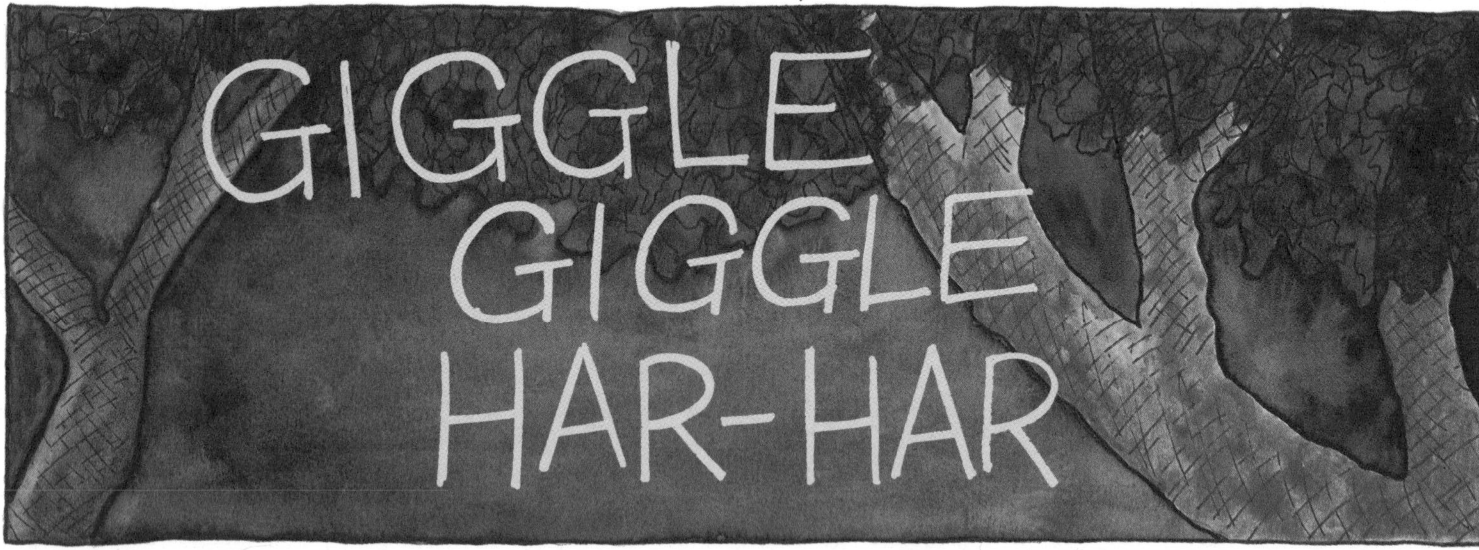
GIGGLE
GIGGLE
HAR-HAR

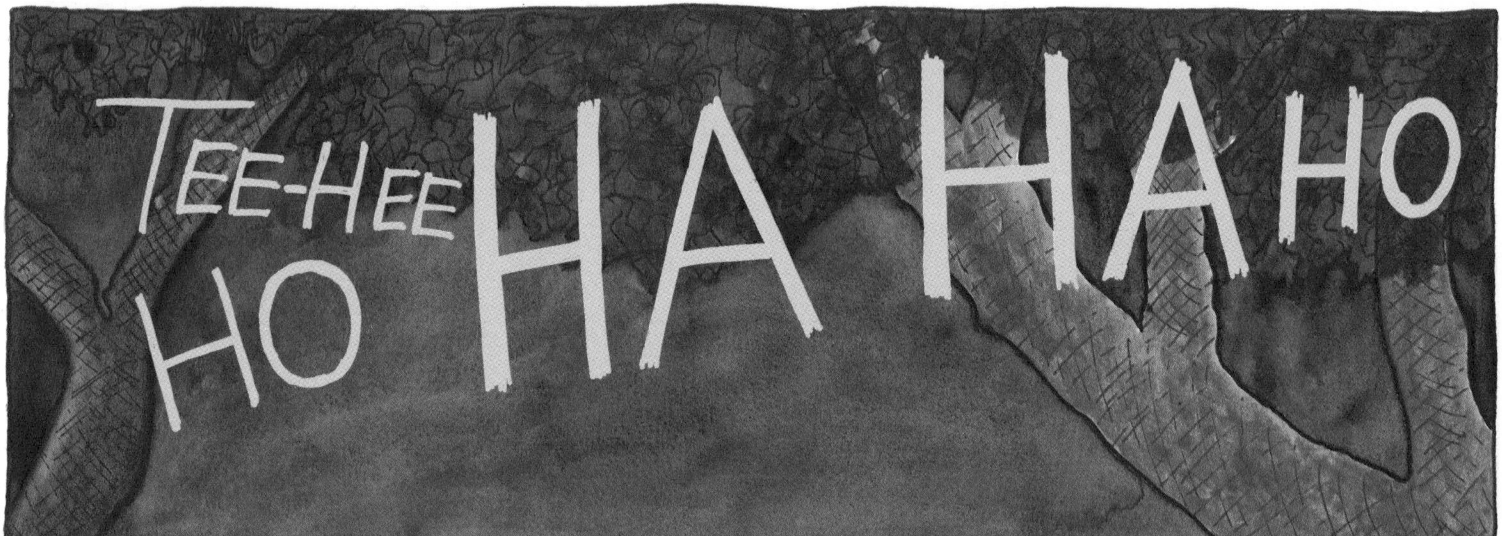
TEE-HEE
HO HA HA HO

Gotta ...

shake, shake, shake my sillies out,

Shake, shake, shake my sillies out,

Shake, shake, shake my sillies out,

And wiggle my waggles away.

Gotta clap, clap, clap my crazies out,

Clap, clap, clap my crazies out,

Clap, clap, clap my crazies out,
And wiggle my waggles away.

Gotta jump, jump, jump my jiggles out,

Jump, jump, jump my jiggles out,

Jump, jump, jump my jiggles out,
And wiggle my waggles away.

Gotta yawn, yawn, yawn my sleepies out,
Yawn, yawn, yawn my sleepies out,

Yawn, yawn, yawn my sleepies out,

And wiggle my waggles away.

Gotta shake,

shake,

shake my sillies out,

Shake, shake, shake my sillies out,

Shake, shake, shake my sillies out,

And wiggle my waggles

away.

SHAKE MY SILLIES OUT

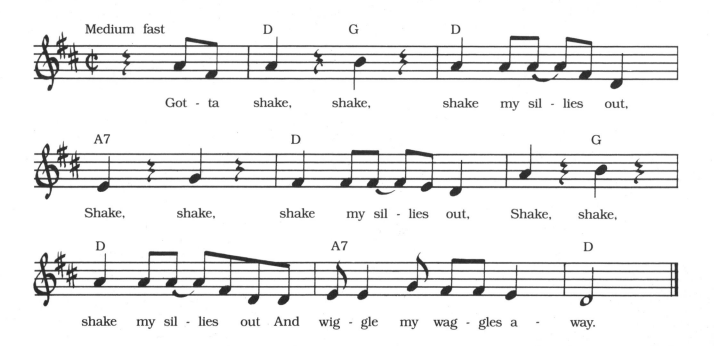